Signs of
Emotional Abuse:
How to Recognize the Patterns
of Narcissism, Manipulation, and
Control in Your Love
Relationship

Barrie Davenport

ISBN-10:1540707377
ISBN-13:9781540707376

Disclaimer

the United States, Canada, or any other jurisdiction is the sole responsibility of the purchaser or reader.

Neither the author nor the publisher assumes any responsibility or liability whatsoever on the behalf of the purchaser or reader of these materials.

Any perceived slight of any individual or organization is purely unintentional.

Your Free Gifts

As a way of saying thank you for your purchase, please begin this book by taking my Emotional Abuse Test to help you clarify if you are in an emotionally abusive relationship. Many people are confused about whether or not certain behaviors qualify as abusive. This assessment covers the specific behaviors and language that emotional abusers use consistently.

You can download your assessment and get your personal score by going to this site:

http://liveboldandbloom.com/emotional-abuse-test

As a second gift, please enjoy my free ebook, *Encouragement and Advice from Emotional Abuse Survivors.* This book offers insights on how to improve your self-esteem and inner strength from 65 women and men who are members of my Emotional Abuse Breakthrough Facebook Support Group.

You can download the ebook by going to this site:

http://liveboldandbloom.com/65-survivors.

Contents

About Barrie Davenport

Barrie Davenport is a certified personal coach, thought leader, author, and creator of several online courses on emotional abuse, self-confidence, life passion, habit creation, and self-publishing.

She is the founder of two top-ranked personal development sites, LiveBoldandBloom.com and BarrieDavenport.com. Her work as a coach, blogger, and author is focused on offering people practical strategies for living happier, more successful, and more mindful lives. She utilizes time-tested, evidence based, action-oriented principles and methods to create real and measurable results for self-improvement.

You can learn more about Barrie on her Amazon author page at barriedavenport.com/author.

Introduction

"Is it really abuse?"

"Am I overreacting?"

"Could it be my fault?"

Victims of emotional abuse often are confused about whether or not their partner's behavior is really abuse.

They know something is off. They know they're in a lot of pain. But all too often, victims are reticent to call what's happening in their relationship "abuse." In fact, they are quick to blame *themselves* for their partner's behaviors, or they look for logical reasons why this person who was once loving and kind (and may still be from time to time) can behave so hurtfully.

Some victims have never heard the term "emotional abuse," or if they have, they dismiss it as a pop psychology buzz phrase that doesn't apply to them. They assume abuse occurs only when physical violence is involved. Unless their partner is throwing a punch, shoving them around, or slapping them across the face, everything else is fair game. The controlling behaviors, manipulation, verbal assaults, and mind games all appear to be normal and acceptable conduct in an intimate relationship.

In my Emotional Abuse Breakthrough Facebook Support Group (see Support Resources), I often see comments that reflect this confusion:

> *My husband yells at me and calls me the worst names imaginable when he gets upset. He tells me I'm not smart enough to manage our money, so he controls all the finances. I have to ask his approval to go buy clothes for the kids and myself. Whenever I complain about it or tell him I want him to stop being so controlling, he twists it all around saying I'm being selfish and controlling. But sometimes he can be really sweet and act like nothing's wrong. Is this really abuse? Don't all couples fight about money and yell at each other? Maybe I'm being too sensitive.*

The answer to this frequently asked question, "Is this really abuse?" is a resounding "Yes." Emotional abuse is abuse, and it is devastating to the victim. It can cause deep and lasting psychological trauma and is often the precursor to physical violence. It is a serious and often misunderstood relationship dynamic that can completely destroy marriages and intimate connections. It is real, it's wrong, and unfortunately it occurs in far too many relationships.

As I mention in my book *Emotional Abuse Breakthrough,* "A 2007 study of Spanish college students between the ages of 18–27 found that emotional abuse is so widespread in dating relationships that it's seen as a normal part of dating." A normal part of dating? How is it these behaviors are so entrenched in *courtship,* the time when you are at your best with a new love interest, that they are considered normal?

According to the National Coalition Against Domestic Violence (NCADV), "Psychological abuse involves trauma to the victim caused by verbal abuse, acts, threats of acts, or coercive tactics. Perpetrators use psychological abuse to control, terrorize, and denigrate their victims. It frequently occurs prior to or concurrently with physical or sexual abuse." Psychological abuse in intimate relationships is not an infrequent occurrence.

An NCADV report offers these statistics:

- 48.4% of women and 48.8% of men have experienced at least one psychologically aggressive behavior by an intimate partner.

- 4 in 10 women and 4 in 10 men have experienced at least one form of coercive control by an intimate partner in their lifetime.

- 17.9% of women have experienced a situation where an intimate partner tried to keep them from seeing family and friends.

- 18.7% of women have experienced threats of physical harm by an intimate partner.

• 95% of men who physically abuse their intimate partners also psychologically abuse them.

• Women who earn 65% or more of their households' income are more likely to be psychologically abused than women who learn less than 65% of their households' income.

Emotionally abusive behaviors are so prevalent with couples that one might assume they are typical and even acceptable ways of relating and interacting. But emotional abuse is far from acceptable or healthy. It wreaks havoc on the victim's mental health, particularly female victims.

Again, according to the National Coalition Against Domestic Violence, "7 out of 10 psychologically abused women display symptoms of PTSD [posttraumatic stress disorder] and/or depression," and further, "Psychological abuse is a stronger predictor of PTSD than physical abuse among women."

Emotional abuse happens with couples around the world—whether they are rich and poor, gay or straight, educated or uneducated, confident or insecure. Men can be abusers, but women can also practice abusive behaviors with their male or female partners. An abuser's behaviors so infect their victim/partner that he or she can become abusive as well.

It's not uncommon for both victims and abusers to have experienced childhood abuse or neglect, and they repeat the pattern learned in their youth within their current relationship. However, people from healthy, happy childhood families can also find themselves in an emotionally abusive intimate relationship as adults. Emotional abuse doesn't discriminate.

Often when a romantic relationship begins, the abuser is attentive, charming, and kind. Perhaps he's a little jealous, but initially it seems flattering and sweet that he can't stand the thought of another guy's attention. Maybe she's a bit needy, but it's endearing that she depends on you so much. Over time, the jealousy, neediness, and endearing behaviors turn ugly and controlling. The charm drops away to reveal a darker, angrier, more manipulative personality. The person who was once so attentive has turned from Dr. Jekyll into Mr. or Mrs. Hyde.

Says one emotional abuse victim, "I had early warning signs, and I did question him over these things, but he always had an answer, then would give me his hard-luck stories about his life so I would feel sorry for him, so I stayed, as I felt he needed me."

This is classic emotional abuser behavior. There is always an excuse, an explanation, a hard-luck story—and the victim is quick to forgive and move on, hoping the behavior is a one-off lapse that won't happen again.

However, emotional abusers don't change on their own, and their outbursts and bad behaviors aren't occasional. This abuse isn't simply a slip-up, an isolated incident, or a sudden loss of control. It is a *consistent pattern* of behavior that reflects an attitude of entitlement, disrespect, and intentional manipulation.

The longer the victim allows the behavior to continue unchecked, the more confident and controlling the abuser becomes. The abuser attempts to confuse and obfuscate to keep his or her partner off-balance and constantly wondering about their own sanity or judgment. If you are uncertain about whether or not you're being emotionally abused, it's likely your abuser is working hard to keep you in that state of confusion.

Eventually, confusion turns to despair, hopelessness, depression, and anxiety. You feel powerless to take action and completely under the thumb of this so-called love partner who doesn't seem to care that he or she is destroying your self-esteem and happiness.

The Power of Awareness

The first step to all change is awareness. You can't pretend, ignore, excuse, or deny and have any hope of improving your relationship, your mental health, or your quality of life. You must look at emotional abuse for exactly what it is: selfish, abusive, cruel behavior that is unacceptable, inexcusable, and intolerable in your life moving forward.

Just to be clear, so there is no equivocation or confusion, emotional abuse is an *ongoing pattern* (not a one-off occurrence) of behavior and words meant to systematically diminish and confuse you, so the abuser can exert more and more power to bring you to submission. The behaviors occur daily or weekly, and, more often than not, you feel hurt, confused, controlled, angry, unloved, and alone. After years of abuse, these feelings turn into depression and generalized anxiety.

Facing the truth about emotional abuse is painful and scary. It's heartwrenching to realize the man or woman you love is an abuser who would treat you so abominably. It's tormenting to acknowledge that you may need to end the relationship for your own sanity or spend months or years in counseling (assuming your abuser will go) to work through the pain and repair the connection.

For many victims, the anxiety associated with standing up to the abuser and calling him or her out on the abuse is overwhelming and debilitating. The fear of the abuse escalating is enough to make you bury your head in the sand and pretend everything is perfectly fine. But deep down, you know it's not. Deep down, part of you is dying.

If you're reading this book, you know something is wrong. But this glimmer of awareness reveals that you have the inner strength and a longing to figure out what the hell is going on and what you can do about it. Even though you may feel scared and insecure, part of you wants to know the truth and face up to it. It may feel like pulling the thread that could unravel your entire life—but you know you have to pull it.

Recognizing the signs of emotional abuse will empower you to know what you're dealing with and whether or not your partner is truly an abuser. You may not be ready today or next week or next month to take action—but knowledge gives you power and confidence. As this information sinks into your psyche, it will be hard to simply move on and accept your partner's bad behaviors. At some point, you will be called to step up and demand change.

It is my hope that this book will be the first step toward empowering yourself to take action, as well as recognizing that you are worth so much more than the treatment you're receiving from your abusive partner.

For now, I invite you to look at your relationship with the cool detachment of an investigator. Step back from your hopes and dreams about your partner. Step back from your pain and frustrations. Step back from the shock and disbelief that this is happening to you. Simply look at the facts, and compare those facts with what you believe to be acceptable, loving, trustworthy, supportive, respectful words and actions in an intimate relationship.

As you read through these 125 signs of emotional abuse in the nine patterns outlined in this book, ask yourself these questions:

- Does my partner exhibit these behaviors (or similar behaviors)?

- Does it happen on a regular basis (daily or weekly)?

- Do the behaviors or words hurt, anger, confuse, embarrass, manipulate, or shame me?

- Is my mental health suffering as a result of my partner's words and behaviors?

- Are these behaviors what I really want in my love relationship?

- Would I use this behavior or these words with someone I love?

- How would I react if someone treated my son or daughter the way my spouse treats me?

Your partner doesn't have to exhibit all 125 behaviors to be emotionally abusive. Just one or two of these behaviors inflicted regularly is enough to qualify as abuse. You may notice your partner has his or her own brand of abuse and exhibits regular patterns of select behaviors. She may be verbally abusive but never make threats or have unpredictable behavior. He may be demanding and selfish, but he doesn't gaslight you or play mind games. Some abusive partners may practice a wide variety of behaviors from many of the nine patterns of abuse.

If you reach the conclusion that your spouse or partner is emotionally abusive, your next questions will naturally be, "Now what? How can I fix this, or change it, or end it? Can my partner change and stop abusing me? Is our relationship over or can it work?"

I'd like to invite you to read my other books on emotional abuse to help you navigate your next steps: *Emotional Abuse Breakthrough: How to Speak Up, Set Boundaries, and Break the Cycle of Manipulation and Control with Your Abusive Partner* and *Emotional Abuse Breakthrough Scripts: 107 Empowering Responses and Boundaries to Use with Your Abuser.*

Also, if you are the victim of physical violence or suspect it could happen, you must seek professional assistance right away for your own safety and the safety of anyone living in the home with you, particularly your children.

Please contact a local abuse hotline, a licensed counselor, or the police as soon as possible. You can also contact the National Domestic Violence Hotline at 1-800-799-SAFE (7233) or for the deaf or hard of hearing, contact 1-800-787-3224 (TTY). Your life really could depend on it.

Let's move on to the common signs and patterns of emotional abuse. You don't need to recognize all these signs in order for emotional abuse to be present in your relationship. You may find that your partner focuses on one or two of the nine patterns outlined here.

You may also discover that you are exhibiting some of these signs yourself. As mentioned previously, emotionally abusive behaviors are contagious. Lashing back at your abuser, or even at your children, is a common coping mechanism. Be honest with yourself about this possibility, and use this opportunity to work on yourself, even if you can't change your abuser right away.

Signs of Emotional Abuse

Signs and Patterns of Emotional Abuse

Dominating and Controlling Words and Behaviors

It didn't happen right away. At first, you thought your partner was being overly attentive and helpful. She just wanted the best for you. He's a strong, decisive man who knows what he wants and says what he means.

But as time went by, the suggestions and friendly tips morphed into criticisms and demands. The charm turned into manipulation, and his kindness hinged on your toeing the line. It turns out, your perfect lover is a control freak who demands that everything is his way or the highway.

Sometimes this control is subtle, like giving you a nasty look, but other times it is more overt and frightening, like cursing and yelling at you.

The controlling, dominating abuser has an array of psychological tools at her disposal to ensure you do what she wants or suffer the consequences. The consequences range from ultimatums, manipulations, and threats, to shaming, blaming, and shutting you down.

Here are some of the signs of domination and control you might recognize.

1. Shows boredom when you talk, using crossed arms, head down, and deep sighs.

Everything about your partner's demeanor suggests that he or she has no use for what you are saying or doing. Body language speaks volumes, and the message is loud and clear here: "If you don't shut up, I'm shutting you out."

2. Says things to upset or frighten you.

Maybe you are tender-hearted, sensitive, or easily upset. Your abusive partner has found your Achilles heel and is playing you for all it's worth. If you don't obey, go along, or toe the line, your partner is going to threaten and scare you into it.

3. Becomes overly and inappropriately jealous of attention from or conversation with others.

Your partner doesn't like the idea of sharing you with anyone—even in the most innocuous, innocent situations. He or she will make sure you never cross the line again by inflicting the pain of extreme jealous tantrums and threats.

4. Presumes you are guilty until you are proven innocent.

Rather than seeing you in the best light possible and assuming you have good intentions and judgment, your abusive partner begins with a presumption of guilt. You are forced to win your case in order to maintain his or her goodwill and faith in you.

5. Intentionally makes you so tired of arguing that you relent.

Some abusers can and will argue endlessly. While you are exhausted and drained, he or she seems energized by fighting and pushing your buttons. They know you will eventually give in from sheer exhaustion.

6. Constantly "keeps score" to coerce you into doing what he or she wants.

Your abusive partner knows exactly how many times who has done what and who owes whom. But it appears you are the one who is always in debt. If your abuser wants you to do something, he will dredge up some slight from the past or some "big favor" he's done for you to guilt or shame you into action.

7. Makes you do humiliating or demeaning things.

Her dog has once again pooped on the carpet, but somehow it's your fault, and you have to clean it up. He's not pleased with the waiter's service, so he demands you both storm out of the restaurant after yelling at the poor server and humiliating you. You need the keys to the car, but he's pissed you're going out, so he throws them across the room for you to "fetch" like a dog.

8. Makes you "earn" trust or kind treatment.

All you want is to be treated with respect and kindness, but respect and kindness are conditional with your abusive partner. Maybe it doesn't come until you have sex every night, buy her that new car she wants, or give in to his demands for control over everything. There's always a hoop to jump through before you are treated with decency.

9. Keeps you "in debt" with gifts, meals, etc., so you are beholden to him or her.

At first, you thought he or she was the most generous, thoughtful person on the planet. You were showered with gifts and kindnesses that made you feel so special—until you realized a condition was tied to each gift. When you don't comply to your abuser's demands, you hear about every gift and every gesture, with a reminder of the debt you have yet to pay off.

10. Gives you disapproving or contemptuous looks or body language.

You know your partner all too well, and he or she doesn't have to say much to get you to toe the line. You know that once his eyebrow begins to furrow or her arms start to cross, things can get really ugly. You've been trained by the slightest shift in

expression or adjustment of the body that you
better back down quickly or prepare for a blowup.

**11. Views you as an extension of himself or
herself, rather than an individual.**

You so long to be number one in your partner's life
that you'd do just about anything to get his or her
attention and have an emotional connection. And
your partner is keenly aware of that. Either your
partner doesn't view you as a worthy individual
deserving of respect, or she sees that taking
advantage of your need to be acknowledged is a
great way to control you.

12. Monitors your time and whereabouts.

Nothing is more controlling and dominating than
someone checking up on you constantly and
managing what you do and where you go.
Emotional abusers are masters at monitoring you
and will either guilt you into staying put or threaten
you if you step out of line. As a result, you feel like
you're under house arrest with no freedom or
decision-making powers.

**13. Monitors your telephone calls/texts or email
contacts.**

This kind of monitoring is just another way of
controlling you and crossing your personal
boundaries. You feel like a child whose parent
suspects you're up to no good—except you aren't a
child. You're an adult with a right to privacy and a
right to contact whomever you wish without
interference.

14. Snoops in your personal belongings, purse, wallet, etc., to violate your privacy.

The message here is that what's yours is his, and he can do whatever he wants because he "owns" you and your property. He or she believes that since you are a couple, there are no privacy boundaries—at least with you. But the same rules don't apply to your abuser who would freak out if you snooped in his things.

15. Defends monitoring and snooping, suggesting you shouldn't mind if you have nothing to hide.

Rather than acknowledge that snooping and monitoring is a violation of your privacy and basic rights as an adult, your abuser tries to turn the tables to make it your fault. Your anger at this violation is clearly an indicator that you have something to hide. The abuser hopes to confuse and shame you into allowing the behavior to continue.

16. Makes decisions that affect both of you or the family without consulting you or reaching agreement with you.

An emotional abuser will attempt to put you in a secondary (or bottom-rung) position in the family by neglecting or refusing to include you in important decisions. He doesn't want his position of power to be usurped or undermined if you have a differing opinion. She doesn't really see you as an equal decision maker in the family, so why even consult you? Eventually you forget how to make decisions and rely on your abuser to manage things.

17. Withholds resources, such as money.

If you have no means of getting help, standing up for yourself, leaving the relationship, or demanding your rights, then your abuser has gained the ultimate control. It's hard to hire a counselor, retain a lawyer, buy your own car, or open a bank account when your abusive partner manages and controls all the money.

18. Restricts your usage of the telephone and/or car.

The abuser uses his psychological and sometimes physical power to prevent you from making calls or driving in order to get support or help. Perhaps he has threatened you and made you believe that if you try to leave or get help, you'll lose your children, your house, your money, or even your physical safety.

19. Won't allow you to leave the house alone.

If you are allowed to leave, it always has to be with your abuser or an "abuser approved" person who will report back on your actions and behaviors. You don't feel safe emotionally to leave the house alone because you fear the consequences from your partner.

20. Prevents you from working or attending school.

If you try to improve yourself, boost your self-esteem, or empower yourself in any way, your abuser makes it impossible. He doesn't want you to have your own money or improve your education enough that you might have financial freedom and independence. He wants you completely dependent on him.

21. Prevents you from socializing with friends and/or seeing family.

Your close friends and family are often the first to see the abuse going on with your partner, and because they care for you, they are often the first to speak up. Once your partner realizes these people see the abusive dynamic, he will do everything in his power to prevent you from spending time with these friends and family.

22. Prevents you from seeking medical care or other types of help.

Maybe you've had anxiety attacks, depression, or even physical ailments as a result of this abusive relationship. You need to see a doctor or counselor for help, but your abusive partner sees this as a potential threat and stands in the way of your seeking treatment. You might have the flu, a sprained ankle, or some other medical situation that requires attention, but your abuser demands you tough it out for fear you might reveal the abuse to an authority figure or medical professional.

Verbal Abuse

Verbal abuse is almost always present in emotionally abusive relationships. Words and tone of voice are used to threaten you, frighten you, embarrass you, and keep you off balance. Verbal abuse often involves yelling, cursing, name-calling, bullying, and suggestions of future physical violence.

However, verbal abuse doesn't have to be as overt or dramatic. It can involve more subtle tactics where the abuser twists language and words so you're not really sure of the meaning or intent. The words are often so convoluted and disconcerting that you're reticent to call it out or take action against it. The abuser wants you to believe you're imagining it or even the cause of it.

Whether it's openly aggressive or more covert, verbal abuse is tremendously damaging to your self-esteem. When someone chronically uses their words to put you down, control, or manipulate you—and then they deny it—they become true verbal abusers. The goal, whether or not the abuser recognizes it, is to gain dominance and control over you.

Here are some of the signs of verbal abuse you might recognize.

23. Yells at you.

The trigger can be anything from forgetting to pick up the laundry to giving her the wrong look. Everything can be peaceful and calm one minute, and then the next minute your abusive partner is yelling at the top of his or her lungs. If this has happened more than once, your partner realizes how much you dislike yelling and how quickly you'll back down when he raises his voice. Yelling has become the standard operating procedure for getting you, and even your kids, to take action and take it quickly.

24. Insults you.

Your abusive partner's form of verbal abuse might include some select phrases to insult you and put you down. Maybe you've been called stupid, fat, lazy, slutty, or worthless. Maybe you've been called worse. Abusers know that the more they insult you, the more you begin to believe these negative things about yourself. As your self-esteem erodes, your abuser gains more and more power.

25. Threatens you.

Fear is a huge motivator, and your abuser uses it to get his or her way. If you don't comply with your abuser's wishes, you are threatened with loss of your security, house, children, finances, and safety. The threats may be direct or subtle, but either way, the message is loud and clear.

26. Constantly interrupts you or talks over you.

Verbal abusers don't see the need to be polite or respectful in conversation with you. They will dominate the conversation by interrupting you, talking over you, or tuning you out. Your opinions and feelings mean little, and this bully will run over you with loud and rude language to make sure you know who is in charge.

27. Shows complete disregard and disrespect.

Everything about your abuser's words and language reveals his or her contempt for you. Maybe she talks down to you or laughs at you. Maybe he starts humming or looks at the newspaper while you're trying to talk. Your abuser's words and actions when you speak tell you volumes: you are worthless in his or her eyes.

28. Makes "jokes" at your expense.

Both you and your abusive partner know the intent of the "joke." She isn't kidding when she makes fun of your latest job setback in front of her parents. You can feel the edge in his humor when he jokes about your weight gain. Cruelty and disrespect are masked with humor, but you see through it clearly and know your abuser is twisting the knife to make you feel bad about yourself.

29. Uses sarcasm or "teasing" to put you down or make you feel bad.

Sarcasm is using words that mean the opposite of what you really want to say in order to insult, demean, or show irritation. Your abuser might say she is teasing, but you know the truth behind the words. Sarcasm, when used by an abuser, is a passive-aggressive behavior that allows the abuser to pretend as though his or her words were meant jokingly. It's an attempt to keep you off balance and uncomfortable enough that you'll back off.

30. Swears at you or calls you names.

Just like insults and threats, swearing and name-calling is a base attempt to frighten and demoralize you. Unlike the more covert abuse method of sarcasm, swearing and name-calling is about as direct as your abuser can get. He or she has so little respect for you and for common decency that saying offensive, derogatory things is not beneath them. Once you've been called these names enough, you begin to believe them and accept the behavior as normal.

31. Belittles, insults, or ridicules you.

By putting you down and trying to make you feel small and unworthy, your abuser is attempting to empower himself. Rather than viewing you as an equal and worthy of praise, support, and respect, your abusive partner belittles you to disempower you and chip away at your self-worth. The lower you feel, the more control he or she has.

32. Mimics, invalidates, or patronizes you.

When your abuser talks down to you, mimics your words, and diminishes your feelings, she is attempting to invalidate your thoughts, emotions, and beliefs. By doing this, the abuser can pretend that your feelings are meaningless, immature, or unfounded. In the abuser's mind, only his or her opinions and feelings really matter.

33. Makes derogatory comments about a group you belong to.

You may be part of a group of friends, a business organization, a club, or a religious group that is meaningful to you and allows you to express yourself independently of your abuser. Once your abuser gets wind of this, he will attempt to undermine and ridicule the group in an attempt to pull you away from it or make you feel guilty about being part of it.

34. Makes negative comments about people, places, or things that you love.

Anything that is important to you is fair game for the abuser's verbal assaults. The abuser doesn't want you to have friends, interests, or activities that might enlighten you to your own worthiness or reveal the true nature of your abuser's behaviors. He doesn't want you associating with people who feel threatening to his control over you.

35. Dismisses your feelings, thoughts, and experiences on a regular basis.

"You're too sensitive." "Just get over it." "You're acting like a crazy person." "That's not what happened." These kinds of dismissive comments are an attempt to diminish your essential self by making you question your emotions, judgment, and even reality. Not only does your abuser not listen to you, but she invalidates you by telling you that you're wrong and misguided. It makes you question everything about yourself.

36. Trivializes what is important to you.

Rather than offering praise, supportive words, and true interest in topics, people, or events that are important to you, your abuser makes light of them. "Why are you so interested in that movie? It's totally stupid." "You're never going to be a real artist, so why do you keep trying?" Because your partner's good opinion of you is something you long for, his or her diminishing words are like throwing ice water on your enthusiasm and joy. If your own spouse can't support you, then why even try?

37. Sexually devalues you.

Emotional and physical intimacy are intricately wound together. When your partner treats you like a sex object, puts you down sexually, says that you aren't attractive enough, or suggests you aren't performing up to par, then you begin to feel sexually inadequate. This inadequacy translates from the bedroom into all aspects of your relationship. Emotional intimacy and trust are destroyed when your abuser devalues you sexually.

38. Creates circular, neverending conversations to confuse and exhaust you.

Some abusers seem to thrive on stirring the pot with exhausting, circular arguments. They can go on and on with confusing, long-winded tirades that ultimately leave you so exhausted, you give up. You will say or do just about anything to avoid getting trapped in this vortex of confusion and contention—and that's exactly what your abuser wants.

39. Verbally abuses your child or children to hurt you.

It's one thing for your abuser to say hurtful, controlling things to you, but it's another to watch it happen to your children. Your abuser may recognize that you'll do anything to protect your kids from his or her vitriolic, wounding diatribes. So to get you to bend to his will, he'll lash out at your kids. Often the abuser suggests it's your fault. "I'm sorry kids, but if Dad hadn't been so mean, I wouldn't have gotten angry at you."

40. Uses your past secrets or private information against you to wound you.

Your spouse or partner knows more about your private life than just about anyone, and he or she should be your number one protector. Your love partner should hold your private information with respect and dignity. But an abuser sees your private information as yet another way to manipulate and control you. She will either threaten to use it against you, or throw it in your face as a way to wound you.

Demanding and Selfish Expectations

Your emotionally abusive partner is far more focused on his or her needs and wants than yours. In fact, she doesn't have much respect for your time and life priorities, especially if they conflict with hers. The expectation is that you put your abusive partner first, even if it means inconveniencing yourself.

Many emotional abusers view themselves as the dictator of the home. They think they are so above you and your children that they are excused from housework, childcare, or other tasks they find beneath them or simply don't want to deal with. They require you to handle everything, or they passively leave it in your hands by refusing to participate.

These abusers often need regular praise and attention from you to boost their egos and reinforce their power. But you will rarely receive the same attention from them. They can't or won't recognize your emotional needs or respond to your requests for support. If you point this out, the abuser will suggest *you* are being selfish or unloving.

Here are some of the signs of demanding and selfish expectations you might recognize.

41. Expects you to talk to him or her, while you're watching TV, reading, or game playing.

It doesn't matter that you might be busy or engaged in something important to you. Your partner will interrupt you when it suits him. If you don't respond quickly, she might turn the TV off while you're watching or yell to really get your attention. He might pout or claim that you don't love him, or use other passive aggressive means to make you focus on him.

42. Orders you around and treats you like a servant.

"The sink is full of dirty dishes. Get up and clean them right now." "Make me a sandwich. I'm hungry." "I'm tired of listening to the kids' whining. Do something about it." You aren't treated like an equal adult in your own home. You've been relegated to the position of server-in-chief. You jump when your spouse says jump.

43. Gets extremely angry when he or she doesn't get demands met.

If you don't jump when your abusive partner tells you to, you'll pay for it. The consequences might include yelling, cursing, door slamming, pouting, or put-downs. He will make you so anxious or uncomfortable that being a servant seems like the best alternative.

44. Is excessively sloppy or lazy and expects you to take care of it.

She'll fix herself a meal and then leave her mess for you to clean up. He'll pile his dirty clothes on the floor and yell at you for not washing them. You'll come home from a ten-hour work day to find the house a disaster, but your partner is full of excuses and reasons why she's too busy to help. He'll invite all his friends over for the game, but you're in charge of putting the house in order once they all leave, while he continues to watch TV.

45. Accuses you of being selfish and lazy.

If you complain to your partner about feeling overwhelmed or unfairly put upon, he or she will quickly turn the tables to blame you. He'll suggest that you don't see how much he does during the day or how hard he works. Or you are being selfish and demanding by expecting her to pick up after herself. The impression is that your perceptions of the situation are wrong, and your frustrations are unfounded.

46. Demands obedience to whims.

Some emotional abusers thrive on the role of being a puppeteer and watching you dance according to the way they manipulate you. Just because they can, your partner will ask you to hop up to get something the moment you finally sit down to relax. Because she is too selfish to walk the dog or take out the trash, she demands you handle it every time.

47. Behaves like a spoiled child.

Sometimes it feels like you're living with a toddler or sulky teenager rather than a grown-up. Whining, moaning, pouting, complaining, and temper tantrums are the manipulative tactics of choice for your partner. They attempt to guilt, shame, or frustrate you enough to coerce you into compliance.

48. Acts helpless to get his or her way.

"I just can't cook as well as you do. You need to fix dinner." "The kids never listen to me. You tend to it." "Paying the bills gives me anxiety. You need to handle it." Your abuser feigns helplessness, inability, or dire consequences if he is required to handle normal tasks that he is perfectly capable of handling. It's like pulling teeth to get her help, so you might as well just do it yourself.

49. Gets frustrated or angry when you are sick or incapacitated.

When you are physically or emotionally unable to respond to your abuser's expectations and demands, you rarely receive care, concern, or support. Instead your partner gets angry, shows frustration, or passively allows the house to get dirty, the kids to be untended, or meals to go unprepared.

50. Doesn't tolerate any seeming lack of respect.

As king or queen of the household, your abusive partner expects you to show appropriate respect. That means no questioning, talking back, or standing up for yourself. You will hear about it if you disagree with her opinion or suggest she might be wrong. You'll get an earful if you laugh at him disrespectfully or appear to put him down in front of others.

51. Refuses to share in housework or childcare.

Your partner doesn't passively avoid participating in household responsibilities or dealing with your children. He simply refuses. Taking care of the kids and tending to housework are not his job. Period. It doesn't matter whether you have a fulltime job outside the home—you are in charge of it all if it's going to happen.

52. Has an inability to laugh at himself or herself and doesn't tolerate you or others laughing at him.

Your spouse doesn't find humor in his or her foibles and won't tolerate your pointing out any imperfections, even in lighthearted jest. She doesn't have the ability or the confidence to laugh at herself or be self-deprecating.

53. Acts as though his or her needs supersede your or your children's needs.

This emotional abuser doesn't view you and your family as a team. You are not a partner in the truest sense of the word. You and the kids are the supporting characters in his one-man show. His needs and desires come first, always, even when it's clear you or the kids need support or attention.

54. Exhibits many double standards.

The message is loud and clear: "I'm too good for that, but you're not." Your spouse can sit around and watch hours of TV, but if you do it, you're selfish and lazy. Your partner can yell and curse, but if you raise your voice, you're acting like a bitch or a bastard. This emotional abuser gets carte blanche to do whatever suits him or her, but the same rules don't apply to you.

55. Is unwilling to compromise or negotiate.

You've tried so hard to explain yourself, work out an equitable solution, and make your partner see your perspective. But she's having none of it. It's a "my way or the highway" attitude that makes it clear there is no room for compromise. Even if your partner promises to change, the words are empty, because nothing ever changes.

56. Requires excessive admiration and attention.

You are exhausted by your partner's endless need for praise and attention. She constantly wants to be complimented and built up. His problems and frustrations are always the centerpiece of your conversations. Whatever you have achieved or accomplished, he can out-achieve you. Whatever concerns or challenges you are dealing with, hers are much worse.

Emotional Blackmail

Emotional blackmail is another form of manipulation and control in which your abuser threatens (either overtly or indirectly) to punish you, if you don't comply. Your abuser knows your trigger points, and he or she is adept at taking advantage of them through emotional blackmail tactics.

Emotional abusers know how much you want a real relationship with them. They are keenly aware of your vulnerabilities and your deepest secrets, and early in the relationship, they may have used their charm to get you to share these things. Now they view this knowledge as a powerful tool to use against you and to create the threats that give them the payoff they seek: your full compliance.

There is also an imbalance in the level of self-disclosure between you and your partner. You are open and willing to share, but your partner is more guarded and perhaps secretive. In fact, they are adept at subterfuge and confusion.

In the book, *Emotional Blackmail: When the People in Your Life Use Fear, Obligation, and Guilt to Manipulate You,* authors Susan Forward and Donna Frazier write,

> *"Blackmailers make it nearly impossible to see how they're manipulating us, because they lay down a thick fog that obscures their actions. We'd fight back if we could, but they ensure that we literally can't see what is happening to us"* (page xi).

Knowing how much you want their love and approval, your partner threatens to withhold it or remove it in order to manipulate you. Whatever qualities you value in yourself (kindness, generosity, affection), the emotional abuser will imply that you are lacking in these qualities, if you don't step up. They know how to twist the knife so you feel guilty and shamed into action.

Here are some of the signs of emotional blackmail you might recognize.

57. Escalates abusive language or behavior if you talk back.

Yelling, cursing, and name-calling are deeply offensive to you, and your partner knows it. That's why he resorts to it the minute you give any pushback to his demands. If you want to keep the peace, you better just comply and do what he says.

58. Uses guilt trips or shaming to get his or her way.

"I thought you cared about me? Why won't you do this?" "If you were a real gentleman, you'd be happy to buy me a new car." Any refusal by you is positioned as a character flaw or cruelty. You don't have a right to say "No" without feeling bad about it. Your abuser knows exactly what makes you feel so bad that you'll give in.

59. Behaves dramatically and publicly, until you agree to do what he or she wants.

Nothing is more embarrassing and shameful to you than airing your dirty relationship laundry in public. But your abusive partner doesn't seem uncomfortable at all with it. In fact, she's happy to have a temper tantrum at a restaurant or family gathering in order to get her way. He doesn't mind picking a fight in front of your neighbors if it means you'll acquiesce.

60. Withholds sex or affection to get his or her way.

You crave his physical affection and hugs. You long for the intimacy and connection that you can only find during sex. Yet your abuser has found a way to turn affection and sex into a tool for pressuring you. When you don't submit to his wishes, you get the cold shoulder. Your hugs are pushed away, and your touch is rejected. Unless you finish all the chores and promise to watch the kids for the weekend, you're not going to get any sex.

61. Is frequently emotionally distant or emotionally unavailable.

You frequently find yourself saying, "What's wrong? Is everything OK?" Your spouse has turned as cold as Siberia, and your conversations have become one-word utterances with no effort on her part to show kindness or closeness. You've learned through experience that the only way to melt the iceberg is by yielding to her wishes.

62. Intentionally withholds information that is useful or necessary for you.

Your abusive partner has important information about your kids, your finances, a family event, or any information of value to you or that might impact you. Holding this information is powerful because he or she can use it as a way to make you submit. "As soon as you get this house cleaned up, I'll tell you whether or not I got the raise."

63. Becomes angry or cold when chores are not done when wanted or as wanted.

Your partner is a control freak who requires things to be done just so—and on his or her schedule. If the clothes aren't folded properly, or you neglect to have the garage cleaned out before your family visits, you're going to hear about it. It might be through doors slamming, cursing, or under-the-breath comments about your ineptitude. But you'll know without a doubt that you didn't measure up to expectations.

64. Showers you with approval when you give into him or her and takes it away when you don't.

You've been trained like a puppy to do your partner's bidding. When you follow instructions, you get a pat on the head and extra treats. When you're a bad puppy, you go to the corner of his or her neglect and iciness. It doesn't take long to respond just the way your abuser wants you to.

65. Uses neglect or abandonment to punish or frighten you.

You didn't have dinner on the table fast enough. You came home from work late again. You did something to disrespect your partner, and now you'll pay for it with complete inattention or even your partner's disappearance for a while. She refuses to talk or respond. He decides to take off with his buddies for the weekend without telling you. You become persona non grata until you apologize or change the behavior.

66. Threatens to leave the relationship if you don't give in.

The first few times she said it, you were really hurt and scared. "I'm divorcing you! This relationship is over." When things don't go her way, this threat is now her go-to mantra. Even though the threat is getting old, it doesn't hurt any less. Her loyalty and love is dependent on getting her way.

67. Acts indifferently to your feelings.

No matter how wounded, insulted, offended, shamed, or angry you feel, your partner doesn't seem to care. Your feelings aren't justified and valid. In fact, your emotions are irritating to your spouse. You are overreacting, being ridiculous, or just trying to get attention in your abuser's mind. Your emotions are met with a blank stare or a look of contempt.

68. Shows a general lack of empathy and compassion.

It's not just with you—it's with everyone. Your spouse seems to have little compassion or empathy for the suffering and feelings of others. Only his own feelings really matter in his worldview. She is the only person who has *really* suffered and deserves sympathy (and plenty of it). Whatever concerns or challenges you or others might endure, hers are far, far worse.

69. Threatens suicide if you leave.

Your abusive partner knows how to play on your emotions, because he understands you are a caring, loving person. When all else fails to get your attention or forces you to change your mind about leaving the relationship, he pulls out the big guns— a suicide threat. He knows you don't want that on your conscience, as even the threat of it is enough derail your plans and inner strength.

Unpredictable Behavior

Unpredictable (or protean) behavior is another tactic to intimidate, control, or manipulate you. Protean behavior includes acts that are random and seemingly out of the blue, but sometimes quite calculated and intentional.

The behavior can take many forms, and your abuser knows exactly what to do to keep you off-kilter. Flying into a rage, embarrassing you in public, or throwing things to scare you are common strategies to keep you off balance and anxious.

Your abuser resorts to erratic behaviors in order to keep you confused, so he or she can avoid taking responsibility for his or her own actions. This behavior is a powerful weapon in your abuser's arsenal, as it defies prediction and keeps you walking on eggshells rather than focused on the true challenges in your relationship.

Clinical psychologist Nando Pelusi, in an article for *Psychology Today*, writes, "Erratic behavior served adaptive ends in our past, and it still does. Just as a minnow might cut a zigzagging path to avoid being snapped up by a larger fish, the boss [or your abuser] alternately screams and stonewalls to avoid having her motives laid bare."

The irrationality of your spouse's behaviors can sometimes make you question acceptable and normal adult deportment. What would seem wildly inappropriate coming from a stranger begins to feel tolerable and admissible in your spouse—the person who is supposed to respect you the most.

Here are some of the signs of unpredictable behavior you might recognize.

70. Has unpredictable emotional outbursts.

Screaming. Cursing. A crying jag. Inappropriate laughter. Knocking a lamp off the table. A calm discussion can escalate in a matter of seconds into a full-blown eruption of emotion. You are so caught off guard by this outburst, you have no idea how to respond.

71. Shows a "Jekyll and Hyde" temperament with wild mood swings.

This morning she woke up happy and loving, but by lunchtime she's so cold and rude, you wonder if another person has inhabited her body. One minute he's laughing and having fun with the kids, but the next he's barking out orders and yelling about the dirty dishes. Riding your partner's hourly emotions is like being on a rollercoaster wearing a blindfold. You never know what to expect next.

72. Stomps out of a room during an argument or heated discussion.

You're in the middle of working through a conflict or discussing a serious topic when, out of the blue, she marches out of the room and refuses to talk. Rather than deal with the issue at hand, your partner makes a dramatic (and infantile) exit to show you who's boss and that you're not worthy of a serious, mature conversation.

73. Leaves the house in anger without letting you know where he or she is going.

Your partner slams out the door and drives away in anger. It could be a couple of hours or even a couple of days. You hear nothing from him, and even though you are hurt and angry, you're also consumed with worry. That's exactly the state of mind your abuser hopes to foster in you. The message is clear: "Do what I say, or I'll make you suffer or ignore you altogether."

74. Sulks and refuses to talk about an issue.

Unpredictable behaviors often involve your partner resorting to juvenile performances. You may be discussing an issue like two adults, when suddenly your partner doesn't like the turn of events and decides to pout, scowl, or refuse to talk. You feel like your partner has transformed into an unpleasant teenage version of himself when he can't get his way.

75. Gives the silent treatment and stares you down.

This is yet another childish reaction meant to intimidate or upset you. Your partner wants you to know how upset or angry she is, so rather than forthrightly discussing the matter, she stares you down with an angry smirk or a menacing glare to manipulate you into acquiescing.

76. Shows up unexpectedly drunk or drugged.

Your abuser isn't happy, and things aren't going his or her way. So to get back at you after a fight or to fuel (or muffle) his anger, he starts kicking back the drinks or getting stoned out of his mind. Alcohol and drugs impair your partner's already weak emotional boundaries, and he or she is far more likely to have emotional outbursts in an inebriated state.

77. Throws objects (but not at you), hits or kicks a wall, furniture, doors, etc.

Physical violence, even when it's not directly inflicted on you, is extremely frightening. Your partner has seen how you flinch and cower when he throws things. She knows how much it upsets you when she slams doors or breaks a few dishes to get your attention. It's even more effective when it happens unexpectedly, keeping you perpetually on edge, as you await the next violent outburst.

78. Acts harsh or cruel to pets.

You can see it in your partner's eyes—he really wants to smack you across the face. But rather than hitting you, he takes it out on your pet. He knows how much you love your animal, so he's going to get back at you buy kicking the dog or pretending to put the cat in the oven to scare you.

79. Shakes a finger or fist at you or makes threatening gestures or faces.

He doesn't have to actually slap you for you to feel the sting of his rage. All he needs to do is get in your face and pull back his fist. She doesn't need to lay a finger on you for you to flinch at the look of hatred in her eyes. Real physical abuse feels like it's just a hair's width away from this angry moment, and you truly fear for your safety.

80. Threatens to destroy or actually destroys personal property that belongs to you.

She dangles your cellphone over the toilet, threatening to drop it if you don't apologize right now. He vows to take a golf club to your new car if you cross him one more time. These dramatic threats can catch you completely off guard, and you find yourself scrambling to backtrack so you can protect your valuable property.

81. Threatens to use physical or sexual aggression against you.

The words can be yelled in anger or whispered in a spine-chilling monotone: "I'm going to beat the shit out of you the next time that happens." The seed of violence has been planted, and even if you've never been hit or raped by your abuser, you know the possibility lingers between you.

82. Drives dangerously while you're in the car, as a conscious intentional act to scare or intimidate.

A car can be a dangerous weapon when your partner uses it to frighten you. As the passenger, you are completely out of control, relying on him or her for your physical safety. If he doesn't like the direction of the conversation, he swerves the car toward the guardrail or accelerates to a death-defying speed. The message is clear: "I'm willing to kill us both if you don't comply."

83. Uses your children to threaten you (for example, threatens to kidnap the children).

Nothing is more important to you than the safety and security of your children. That's why your abuser can use them as a pawn in the game she's playing with you. She pulls this card when she really wants to get your attention: "I'll have the kids taken away from you and accuse you of abusing them." Or he might say, "You cross me one more time, and I'm leaving with the kids for good. You'll never see them again."

84. Threatens violence against your children, family, friends, or pets.

Maybe it's not enough to threaten you and your physical safety. Maybe you feel so broken inside that the threats feel empty. But they don't feel empty when they are directed at your loved ones, and your abuser knows it. He will shake you out of any malaise or depression by suddenly suggesting how he might hurt someone you care about.

Chaos and Crisis Creation

Does it seem your partner is fueled and energized by continuous turmoil and drama in your relationship? Is the focus of your life together always on one conflict or crisis after another? Your partner needs to be at the stormy center of attention and will create a tumultuous situation in order to keep things stirred up.

This drama allows your abuser to avoid intimacy and prevents him from confronting his own issues or insecurities. These crises also increase adrenaline, creating a heightened state of arousal that can be an addictive substitute for a real emotional connection with an intimate partner. Knowing that stirring the pot causes you to react with anxiety or fear, your abusive partner uses crisis creation as a way of manipulating you.

Your partner may also have an endless series of problems in other areas of his or her life and always seems at the center of a crisis of some sort. This occurs not just within your relationship, but also at work, with a deadline, with some perceived issue with someone, or with any situation that distracts him or her and drives a wedge in your relationship.

Here are some of the signs of chaos and crisis creation you might recognize.

85. Acts jealous and suspicious of your friends and social contacts.

No matter how innocent, platonic, or wholesome a relationship might be with a friend, coworker, or even family member, your spouse has a way of twisting it into something sordid, selfish, or wrong. She acts out with jealous tantrums or accusatory questions. He's sure your friends are out to get him or tear your relationship apart.

86. Repeatedly crosses your boundaries and ignores requests.

You've asked him to stop groping you in public, but he seems to get off on making you uncomfortable and embarrassing your friends. You've begged her to stop drinking so much at family gatherings, because she always makes an angry scene, but she acts like she never heard your request. It's like she can't wait for the argument at the end of the evening.

87. Acts out to be the center of attention.

It's your child's birthday party, but your spouse makes a big show by wearing a provocative dress and flirting with the other dads. You're in the middle of telling a funny story at a party, and everyone is laughing—except him. He interrupts to tell you that you're telling the story all wrong, and he takes over. Your partner can't stand being on the sidelines of any occasion, especially if you're getting any attention.

88. Makes a big scene about small or insignificant life problems.

The holiday turkey gets burned, and he has to announce what a lousy cook you are in front of the entire family. You forget to bring some important documents to the meeting with the accountant, and she makes sure everyone knows you always make stupid mistakes like this. Your partner trolls through life, looking for reasons to have a blowup and make a scene.

89. Blames you for life difficulties, problems, or unhappiness.

Whatever bad things happen in your abuser's life, whatever difficulties or unhappiness he or she experiences, it's your fault. If he loses his job, it's because you weren't supportive enough. If she's feeling depressed, it's because you don't make her happy. All these negative events are exacerbated by your partner's blame, anger, and negativity.

90. Does something to spite you, just to get a rise out of you.

Your spouse knows you want to be early to get a good seat at your son's basketball game, but she intentionally takes her time getting ready to make you late. The emotional abuser knows what you value and what's important to you, and he or she deliberately undermines your wishes to watch you squirm or gain the upper hand.

91. Ruins birthdays, holidays, or special events with drama, anger, or hurtful behaviors.

No holiday or special event is left untouched by your partner's special form of nasty magic. Rarely does an event go by without a tantrum, emotional outburst, or pouty scene. Your friends and family are starting to avoid time with you and your spouse because of this negativity.

92. Intentionally starts arguments.

You've promised yourself you'll not be drawn in by your partner's constant attempts to pick a fight. But it's hard not to respond to her relentless criticisms, subtle comments, and rude remarks. You can almost see the smile behind his eyes as he awaits your response to his endless nitpicking, hoping you'll fall into his trap of antagonism. It's almost like your partner isn't happy unless he's fighting with you.

93. Compulsively lies or cheats.

You've caught your partner in so many lies, it's hard to keep count of them. And every single time, he denies, denies, denies—and then to add insult to injury, he blames you! You've caught her red-handed texting with another man several times, and she almost dares you to do something about it. Stepping over the line of integrity and trust seems exciting to your abusive partner.

94. Intentionally attacks or demeans things or people important to you to create drama.

He knows how much you love your mom, but you hear him telling your kids what a bitch Grandma is. You've been working for months on planting your garden, but in a fit of rage, she trashes it and pulls out all the plants just as they are taking root. Whatever you value or find pleasure in, your abusive partner takes a weird joy in destroying or undermining it.

95. Pouts, sulks, or acts dramatic to get attention.

Just like a toddler who stomps his feet and rolls on the floor in a tantrum, your spouse pulls out all the stops to get attention—even though it's clear to everyone that the behavior is childish and ridiculous. He or she is not beyond acting like a grown-up baby, if it will provide the distraction and attention desired.

96. Gets inappropriately hysterical.

You announce that you've just been laid off from your job, but your spouse acts like it's all about her. She breaks down, slams doors, and falls apart in heaving sobs. Even though you have barely had time to cope with your own pain and worry, now you have to tend to a hysterical spouse who makes it her drama.

97. Threatens infidelity or divorce to throw you off balance.

Nothing heightens the tension and creates drama like the statement, "There are plenty of men who would treat me much better than you do. I think it's time I find one." Maybe he stirs the pot by announcing, "I'm done with this crap. This marriage is over." Even if you know it's an empty threat, it still feels like a punch in the gut.

98. Threatens to harm himself or herself for attention.

The ultimate, crisis-creation tactic is the threat of suicide or self-harm. If your partner isn't getting the attention or sympathy he or she craves, then why not create a dramatic scene? He announces, "I'm going to swallow the entire bottle of pills. I can't take this life anymore." You are stuck between knowing it's just for show and fearing it might not be this time.

Character Assassination

You are a person of good character most of the time and strive to be kind, gentle, and loving. In fact, abusers often seek out sensitive, giving people for an intimate relationship. The abuser knows that this type of person is eager to please and will prioritize the abuser's needs over their own.

Although your abuser seeks out these character traits in you to serve his purposes, he doesn't relate to them or completely understand them. In fact, the abuser may envy that you have these qualities and he doesn't.

She may observe the positive benefits of your strong character and covet your good qualities. The only way to make herself feel better is to ignore or destroy these qualities. Your abuser's envy forces him or her to devalue the very traits that attracted them to you. He drags your essential character through the mud over every slight or perceived infraction. She finds a way to make your goodness appear trifling and weak.

Your abuser feels the need to put you down and humiliate or embarrass you in front of other people. She undermines your achievements or says ugly things about you behind your back. He might even lie to others about you or try to harm your reputation, if it makes him feel more powerful.

These abusive character attacks can reach a point at which you start to doubt your own good character and lose faith in yourself. The abuser is so adept at twisting things around that you begin to believe the abuser's lies and smears and question your own judgment.

Here are some of the signs of character assassination you might recognize.

99. Belittling, insulting, or berating you in front of other people.

Your spouse or partner waits until there's an audience of people you care about, and then the insults begin. The slights may be subtle or more direct, but everyone in the room feels the tension in the air and knows what's going on. Even if your friends and family don't believe the insults, you feel humiliated and shamed nonetheless.

100. Putting down your physical appearance or intellect.

"When are you going to lose weight? I don't want to be with a fatty." "How stupid can you be? Even a kid knows better than that!" Appearance and intellect are the two easiest targets for an abuser, especially if he feels insecure about his own looks or intellect. If the attacks happen often enough, you begin to feel ugly and stupid. You worry that if you leave the relationship, no one else would ever want you. In fact, your abuser may remind you of that fear frequently.

101. Correcting or chastising you for your behavior.

"I've told you a million times how to fold the laundry the right way. Why can't you get it through your head?" It doesn't matter that you're a full-grown adult, your partner is going to reprimand you like you are a child. It makes her feel powerful and in control of your behavior. It makes you furious to be spoken to this way, but speaking up will only make things worse.

102. Belittling and trivializing you, your accomplishments, or your hopes and dreams.

Whatever successes you've enjoyed, whatever achievements you've obtained, whatever goals you set—your abuser will find a way to minimize them. You won't see pride shining in his or her eyes for your success. Instead, you'll see jealously, contempt, or passivity. The one person whose good opinion matters most to you refuses to give you a morsel of praise or support.

103. Regularly pointing out your flaws, mistakes, or shortcomings.

Rather than acknowledging and appreciating all your good qualities, your spouse has a way of honing in on every mistake you make and every perceived flaw you possess. He knows where you feel shame, vulnerable, or "lesser than," and uses this knowledge as a weapon. During times when your partner feels insecure or angry, he will pick you apart until you begin to feel like you are worthless.

104. Sharing personal information about you with others.

You made the mistake early in your relationship of sharing your most vulnerable fears and personal information. Now your spouse turns this information against you and seems to take pleasure in sharing it with family and friends. She needs confirmation from others that you are a loser and wants to keep you humbled and shamed into doing her bidding.

105. Putting down your friends and/or family.

Your family members and circle of friends are an extension of who you are, and they reflect your inner qualities. So he attacks what's important and valuable to you in order to slam your character and separate you from those you love. "What kind of person would hang around those idiotic friends?" "Your mom is a real bitch. I guess the apple doesn't fall far from the tree."

106. Telling you your feelings are irrational or crazy.

Maybe you are sensitive, sentimental, caring, affectionate, and loving. You might have a soft spot for the pain of others or feel emotions intensely. You might simply want a hug, a calm conversation, a loving response, or a supportive comment. Your abuser isn't capable of showing these emotions or doesn't know how to. So he or she derides you for having them. Your feelings have no value because they make your abuser feel "lesser than."

107. Turning other people against you.

Your abusive partner feels threatened by the positive attention, praise, or love shown to you by others. Rather than feeling proud of you and the way others respond to you, she'll throw you under the bus in front of others or behind your back. She wants to taint your reputation in order to make herself look like the star or to prevent you from having outside influences or distractions.

Gaslighting

Gaslighting is a term that originates from the 1944 movie called *Gaslight,* in which the husband subtly tries to make his wife doubt her perceptions. He tries to convince her (and others) that she's crazy by changing small things (including dimming the gas lights) in their home and elsewhere. When she points it out, he suggests she is mistaken or delusional.

Now the term applies to anyone who tries to manipulate or distort your sense of reality. When your spouse gaslights you, he might deny something that you both know is true or pretend something happened that really didn't. You feel constantly off-balance and filled with self-doubt. "Is it me? Am I going crazy? I know I didn't say that. Or did I?"

He or she might suggest you're lying or exaggerating in an attempt to make you feel stupid or crazy. This is a way to control you or for the abuser to shirk responsibility for his or her actions. But it's a particularly insidious, cruel mental game that corrodes your sense of identity.

Gaslighting calls into question your own good judgment, instincts, and belief in yourself. Once a manipulator gets a foot in the door by making you question your perceptions, he or she will escalate the behaviors to completely extinguish your confidence and self-esteem.

When your abusive partner has undermined your ability to trust your perceptions, you are more likely to stay in the abusive relationship out of fear or insecurity. It feels like only your partner, as hurtful as he or she can be, can understand your "forgetfulness" or your so-called unbalanced behaviors.

Here are some of the signs of gaslighting you might recognize.

108. Accusing you of being "too sensitive" to deflect his or her abusive remarks.

He calls you names, puts you down, and withholds his affection, but when you call him out on it, he pretends he doesn't know what you're talking about. It's YOU who is being too sensitive and overreacting to perfectly normal behavior. You are the difficult partner, not him.

109. Accusing you of being crazy or being the abusive partner.

You know she's lying, manipulating you, and treating you like dirt—or is she? You know you rarely feel loved, but she claims you are off your rails and unappreciative of the good treatment you receive. Any time you push back or question, even just a little, she loses it and claims you're being abusive. You feel completely trapped and confused.

110. Accusing you of lying or having a bad memory.

He comes home with a brand-new sports car and swears the two of you discussed it. You know you didn't. You would never have felt comfortable spending that money on something so frivolous. But he's relentless in claiming he discussed it with you, and you were fine with it. Maybe he did. Maybe you're going crazy. You'd feel so bad if you were wrong about your memory.

Barrie Davenport

111. Hijacking a conversation to confuse or divert the subject away from your needs.

You finally have the courage to express the pain and hurt you're feeling about her abusive behaviors, but before you can get through the first sentence, the conversation has suddenly become all about her. Rather than listening to you, she starts yelling and complaining that you never listen to her and that you only care about yourself. Wait, what's happened here? You've completely lost your train of thought and what you wanted to communicate.

112. Using deceptive communication.

Your abuser has a way of phrasing things that never forthrightly addresses the matter at hand. You rarely get a direct answer to a question. He or she will change the subject to avoid accepting responsibility. She might "neglect" to tell the full story or give the entire truth of a situation. It's subtle enough that it's impossible to call her out on it. If you do, there always seems to be a logical explanation, even when it doesn't seem logical at all.

113. Playing intentional mind games.

Whether it's conscious or not, your partner has an uncanny way of jerking you around with his words. One minute he says he loves you more than anyone, but the next he's pushing you away and refusing your affection. She swears she only has eyes for you, but she waits until you're watching to

57

flirt openly with your neighbor. It's like your partner wants to make you crazy.

114. Blaming you for his or her bad behavior.

He says he wouldn't drink so much if you weren't so demanding. She says that the only reason she yells at the kids is because you don't show her enough love. Whatever your abuser's bad behavior happens to be, *you* are the cause of it. And the argument your partner presents is so compelling, you start to believe it yourself.

115. Accusing or blaming you for things that aren't true, such as infidelity.

You have opened your calendar, your phone, and your computer to your partner to prove your innocence. You've offered to give him proof that you were indeed doing what you said you were doing. But nothing is going to convince him that you aren't lying. You will be accused and blamed, even when it becomes clear you aren't at fault. Logic and truth mean nothing to your abuser.

116. Invalidating or denying his or her emotionally abusive behavior when confronted.

You finally have a handle on what's happening with your partner. You've been reading and learning about emotional abuse, and it's clear your partner is abusing you. You calmly present this to him or her, but the response is complete denial. "I don't do that." "That's not abusive. That's normal for couples." "I've never laid a hand on you, so don't start screaming 'abuse.'" Your abuser accepts zero responsibility for his or her actions, and either blows you off or turns the tables on you.

117. Laughing or smiling at inappropriate situations or during serious conversations.

You want to have a serious conversation with your spouse about how hurt and frustrated you are with his behavior. But during your entire talk, he has a self-satisfied smirk on his face. He looks amused while you're pouring your heart out, and you feel diminished and mocked. He appears to care less about what you have to say. In fact, he thinks it's funny. He laughs in your face, even though you are crying.

Sexual Abuse and Harassment

Subtle sexual harassment and abuse often occurs in emotionally abusive relationships, particularly with male abusers.

Some abusers assume they have sexual "rights" to their partners, whether or not the partner agrees to the sexual encounter. The abuser cajoles, guilt-trips, shames, or does whatever it takes to coerce or cajole the victim into sexual activity. This sometimes includes forced sex.

Although spousal or partner rape is clearly abusive, there are many other forms of sexual harassment and abuse, which can be equally destructive over time.

One of the early warning signs of future sexual abuse is excessive jealousy of other men. Your abuser may view you as a sex object to conquer and dominate, and he assumes all men view you this way.

A sexual abuser frequently says derogatory things about women and will call you and other women names, such as slut, bitch, or whore. His attitude suggests that women are not individuals, but rather sexual objects of derision and possession.

He may laugh at or share jokes portraying women as stupid and unequal to men and will make sexual or crude comments about their appearance, including about his own partner or spouse.

Your abuser might make sexual comments to your female friends and family members in order to degrade you and undermine your friendships with women, further isolating you and making you more dependent on him.

Here are some of the signs of sexual abuse and harassment you might recognize.

118. Makes derogatory or sexual comments about other women's bodies.

"Hey, my wife didn't tell me her best friend was so hot. You should visit us more often." "Your sister's boobs are starting to sag big time. You better not let yourself go like that, or I'm outta here." Your partner has no qualms about comparing your body to another woman's or making inappropriate sexual comments to other women. He will demean other women's bodies or "rate" them in your presence.

119. Shows little or no emotional intimacy during sex.

Your partner does not treat sex as an intimate connection between two loving people. It is an act only meant for his pleasure and physical satisfaction. In sexual encounters, there is little or no foreplay, affection, cuddling, talking, or kissing. He rarely considers your sexual needs or desires.

120. Takes intimate photos or videos of you without your consent (or with coerced consent).

During your most private moments, your spouse wants to take photos or video you, even though you've been clear you're not comfortable doing that. If you say, "No," he begs and cajoles, making you feel guilty or selfish for not meeting his needs. He might even video you without your knowledge or consent, violating your body as well as your trust.

121. Refuses your sexual advances to punish you.

If you reach out to your partner to initiate sex, he or she will push you away and reject you. This refusal isn't merely related to "not being in the mood" or bad timing. It's a calculated tactic to manipulate you into acquiescing to something or a means of punishing you for a perceived slight.

122. Tries to shame or cajole you into having sex.

Maybe you don't feel well. You're tired, or you're busy with a project. Maybe you don't want to have sex because your partner has been hurtful, or you have yet to resolve the last argument between you. But your partner is having none of it. He wants sex now, and he's pulling out all the stops to shame, blame, or guilt you into putting out, regardless of your feelings.

123. Pushes you into sexual acts you don't feel comfortable with.

Everyone has sexual boundaries. There are things they are comfortable with and enjoy, and other acts that feel off limits. However, your partner's limits aren't the same as yours, and even though you've been clear about what you don't want, he won't respect that. He continues to beg, cajole, or even physically push himself on you with acts you loathe.

124. Insults or demeans you sexually or refers to you as a "slut."

His insults don't stop with your appearance or intellect. He has slandered your basic integrity and decency. He says things during or after sex that make you feel like a prostitute or a worthless piece of trash. There's no justification for suggesting you are promiscuous, but to him, it's perfectly acceptable to call you a slut, whore, or worse.

125. Threatens to have affairs, if you don't have sex or perform certain acts.

He wants what he wants in the bedroom, and if he doesn't get it when he wants it, he's made it clear—he'll find it elsewhere. If you don't put out and perform sexually to his expectations, he'll have an affair or find a prostitute to replace you in bed. Your worthiness in the relationship is only as good as your sexual compliance.

Signs of Emotional Abuse

Conclusion

The purpose of this book is to help you have more clarity about your partner's behavior and whether or not it is acceptable and normal in an intimate relationship. If you've asked yourself in the past, "Is my partner abusing me?"—you should now have a much clearer answer. If the answer is "Yes," you may feel more hopeless and despondent than ever. It's painful and embarrassing to acknowledge that the man or woman you love is an emotional abuser. How could this have happened? Why is the person who is supposed to love and cherish you treating you this way?

Sometimes it's easier to stay in the dark and hope that things will get better on their own. Maybe your partner will wake up and see what a great thing he or she has in you and how much love you are willing to give—if only . . .

- If only she would accept your love with gratitude and joy.
- If only he would respond with love, trust, and kindness.
- If only there were a glimmer of willingness from your partner to change the behaviors

and turn back into the man or woman you fell in love with.

With emotional abuse, this transformation rarely happens, without some serious intervention. Most emotional abusers won't have a spontaneous moment of self-reckoning and stop the behaviors. It takes a lifetime and a lot of reinforcement and practice to cultivate these abusive habits. It can take years of highly motivated, sincere effort on your partner's part to change them. Change almost always requires the help and guidance of a counselor trained in working with emotional abuse.

Your partner must acknowledge and admit that he is an emotional abuser. She must want to change and must be willing to accept complete responsibility for her actions. He or she must learn a brand-new way of relating to you in your relationship—and practice it consistently without making excuses for setbacks.

Whether or not this happens with your abuser, *you* need to determine your own next steps. With this new awareness comes the charge to take personal responsibility for your mental health and happiness. Your abusive partner is not invested in your happiness—at least not as much as he is in his own. Only you can take the actions to make your life better.

You may not be in a position (or even want) to leave the relationship right now. But you can manage the abuse, set your boundaries, and begin to stand up for yourself before you sink further into anxiety, depression, and despair. Doing nothing only reinforces the abusive patterns and the toxic dynamic between you and your spouse or partner.

As confused, anxious, and insecure as you may feel right now, you do have some power in your relationship. It may feel like your partner holds all the cards to your happiness, but that's not entirely true. Once you step out from under the fog of your previous confusion and uncertainty, you'll be able to see what your options are and determine the actions you are willing to take to protect yourself, reclaim your power in the relationship, and rebuild your confidence.

I encourage you to take the next step in furthering your understanding of emotional abuse and how it is impacting you, your children, your friends and family, and every aspect of your life. Educate yourself on the damage that emotional abuse is doing to you, and why you need to take steps as soon as possible to stop it.

Learn what an emotionally healthy, mature, loving, respectful relationship entails, and what your personal values are when it comes to the behaviors and words you find acceptable in a relationship. Work on building your confidence, your inner strength, and your sense of self-worth that has been diminished by your partner.

If you'd like to learn more about emotional abuse and want support in deciding whether to stay in the relationship or leave it, I invite you to read my book, *Emotional Abuse Breakthrough: How to Speak Up, Set Boundaries, and Break the Cycle of*

Signs of Emotional Abuse

Manipulation and Control with Your Abusive Partner (liveboldandbloom.com/eab-book) .

The companion book to *Emotional Abuse Breakthrough* is called *Emotional Abuse Breakthrough Scripts: 107 Empowering Responses and Boundaries to Use with Your Abusive Partner.* This book will help you know what to say to your partner in various abuse situations, without resorting to anger or abusive tactics yourself, and how to speak up confidently during these emotionally charged situations. It also includes ideas for communicating your personal boundaries and implementing consequences if boundaries are crossed. Both books can be invaluable resources for you as you work through the challenges you face in your relationship. I've also listed additional support resources in the next section of this book.

It is my sincere wish for you that you will take this information and your newly found awareness about emotional abuse and use it to change your life and your circumstances. You deserve a relationship with someone who is loving, kind, trustworthy, respectful, and mentally healthy. You should accept nothing less. Although you may feel beaten down and incapable of standing up to your abusive partner in this moment, you have more strength than you might think.

Now that you recognize how your partner is treating you and that this treatment is abusive, you might just tap into a reserve of fortitude and resolve that you didn't know you possessed. As author Susan Gale reminds, "Sometimes you don't realize your own strength until you come face to face with your greatest weakness."

Signs of Emotional Abuse

Support Resources

Emotional Abuse Breakthrough Course
(http://emotionallyabused.com/)

Find a Therapist
(https://therapists.psychologytoday.com/rms/)

Breakthrough Behavioral, Inc. online therapy
(https://www.breakthrough.com/)

HelpGuide.org, resource for mental, emotional, and
social health
(http://www.helpguide.org/)

WomensHealth.gov
(http://womenshealth.gov/)

Barrie's Emotional Abuse Breakthrough Facebook
Support Group
(https://www.facebook.com/groups/2863330782000
34/?fref=ts)

The National Domestic Violence Hotline
1-800-799-SAFE (7233)
1-800-787-3224 (TTY)
(http://www.thehotline.org/)

Signs of Emotional Abuse

Childhelp National Child Abuse Hotline
1-800-4-A-CHILD (1-800-442-4453)
(https://www.childhelp.org/hotline/)

Want to Learn More?

If you'd like to learn more about emotional abuse, healthy relationships, confidence, and self-esteem, please visit my blog, Live Bold and Bloom.com, and check out my course, Emotional Abuse Breakthrough at http://emotionallyabused.com/.

Signs of Emotional Abuse

Did You Like *Signs of Emotional Abuse?*

Thank you so much for purchasing *Signs of Emotional Abuse: How to Recognize the Patterns of Narcissism, Manipulation, and Control in Your Love Relationship*

I'm honored by the trust you've placed in me and my work by choosing this book to better understand emotional abuse and the behaviors and words involved in abusive relationships. I truly hope you've enjoyed it and found it useful for your life.

I'd like to ask you for a small favor. Would you please take just a minute to leave a review for this book on Amazon? This feedback will help me continue to write the kind of books that will best serve you. If you really loved the book, please let me know!

Signs of Emotional Abuse

Other Books You Might Enjoy from Barrie Davenport

Emotional Abuse Breakthrough: How to Speak Up, Set Boundaries, and Break the Cycle of Manipulation and Control with Your Abusive Partner
(liveboldandbloom.com/eab-book)

Emotional Abuse Breakthrough Scripts: 107 Empowering Responses and Boundaries to Use with Your Abuser
(liveboldandbloom.com/ea-scripts)

Building Confidence: Get Motivated, Overcome Social Fear, Be Assertive, and Empower Your Life for Success
(liveboldandbloom.com/building-confidence)

Peace of Mindfulness: Everyday Rituals to Conquer Anxiety and Claim Unlimited Inner Peace
(liveboldandbloom.com/mindfulness-post)

Finely Tuned: How to Thrive as a Highly Sensitive Person or Empath
(liveboldandbloom.com/finely-tuned)

201 Relationship Questions: The Couple's Guide to Building Trust and Emotional Intimacy
(liveboldandbloom.com/201-questions)

Self-Discovery Questions: 155 Breakthrough Questions to Accelerate Massive Action
(liveboldandbloom.com/questions-book)

Confidence Hacks: 99 Small Actions to Massively Boost Your Confidence
(liveboldandbloom.com/confidence-hacks)

10-Minute Declutter: The Stress-Free Habit for Simplifying Your Home
(liveboldandbloom.com/10-min-declutter)

10-Minute Digital Declutter: The Simple Habit to Eliminate Technology Overload
(liveboldandbloom.com/digital-declutter)

Declutter Your Mind: How to Stop Worrying, Relieve Anxiety, and Eliminate Negative Thinking
(liveboldandbloom.com/declutter-mind)

Sticky Habits: How to Achieve Your Goals without Quitting and Create Unbreakable Habits Starting with Five Minutes a Day
(http://liveboldandbloom.com/sh-book2)

The 52-Week Life Passion Project: Uncover Your Life Passion
(liveboldandbloom.com/life-passion-book)

Made in the USA
Lexington, KY
05 April 2017